BACKYARD WITCHCRAFT

BACKYARD WITCHCRAFT

The Complete Guide for the
Green Witch, the Kitchen Witch,
and the Hedge Witch

Cecilia Lattari

Illustrations by
Betti Greco

ixia
PRESS

Garden City, New York

Translation: ICEIGeo, Milan (Coordination: Lorenzo Sagripanti;
Translation: Alexa Ahern)

WS White Star Publishers® is a registered trademark property of White Star s.r.l.

Copyright

Bibliographical Note

This Ixia Press edition, first published in 2022, is a modified English translation of *Backyard Witchcraft*, originally published in Italian by White Star Publishers, Milan, in 2022.

The recipes and remedies contained in this publication are not a substitute for professional medical advice. This book is intended for general informational purposes only and does not address individual circumstances. The author and publisher are not responsible for any adverse or allergic reactions to ingredients used throughout this book. Plants and fungi that are deemed poisonous, including derivatives thereof, should not be ingested in any form.

Please exercise caution when performing actions involving candles, incense, and fire. This book is not recommended for children.

Library of Congress Cataloging-in-Publication Data

Names: Lattari, Cecilia, author. | Greco, Betti, illustrator.
Title: Backyard witchcraft : the complete guide for the green witch, the kitchen witch, and the hedge witch / Cecilia Lattari ; illustration by Betti Greco.
Description: Garden City, New York : Ixia Press, 2022. | Includes bibliographical references. |
Summary: "Traditionally, witches have used plants, herbs, and spices in spells, talismans, and potions. In Backyard Witchcraft, Cecilia Lattari guides readers to reawaken their own inner witch by tuning in to natural magic in their everyday lives" —Provided by publisher.
Identifiers: LCCN 2021058668 | ISBN 9780486850047 (trade paperback)
Subjects: LCSH: Witchcraft.
Classification: LCC BF1566 .L39 2022 | DDC 133.4/3—dc23/eng/20220120
LC record available at https://lccn.loc.gov/2021058668

IXIA PRESS
An imprint of Dover Publications

Printed in China
85004803   2023
www.doverpublications.com/ixiapress

—

MAGIC IS A DAILY PRACTICE

✦　✦　✦

We can find magic all around us if we just pay attention. In this chapter, we will get to know the green path, a path that is closely tied to the earth, plants, and nature. We will discover the witches that can be found on this path, from the true green witch to the hedge witch— she who lives at the edge of the woods. The elements, tools, and practices of green magic are special aspects used daily, and this chapter will provide an overview. Part of the introduction is also dedicated to poisonous plants and their magical and lunar path.

EVERY WITCH HAS A GARDEN

+ + +

Even if she doesn't live in the middle of the woods and her house is in the center of a city, a witch always has a garden, with violets growing below her house and in the building's courtyard or blooming dandelions that sprout up along the streets. If the witch lives in the suburbs, she grows marigolds and lavender in recycled vases on the balcony where she observes the moon. Every witch has a garden. I live near the woods, and I thank the wolves, oaks, and chestnuts every day for protecting my garden and plants. I recognize green witches, even if they do not yet know they are one. They have cupboards full of seeds to plant in the spring, or they don't sleep without their evening ritual of herbal tea, sipped under the stars.

Green magic and contact with it are established and expressed in daily life and through one's relationship with nature. Plants are creatures that live in close proximity to humans, and within this intimate relationship the spirituality related to green magic is born. We are used to considering our relationship to plants as unilateral, but it is actually reciprocal. It is important to discover and explore

this relationship. Through our senses and intuition, we can fully get to know a plant. Spending time with a plant that we like, taking care of it and discovering how it grows are perfect ways to start on the green path. You don't have to live in the woods to come into contact with plants and the natural world.

The witch and her garden have a close bond, and they learn from each other. A garden—whether it's a true botanical garden or just a little patch of land, balcony, terrace, or windowsill—can teach us slowness, a perception of changing seasons, a sense of cyclical time, which is how a witch lives and works. The changing seasons are related to our internal clock, and they remind us that everything ends before it comes back transformed. The garden teaches the witch how important it is to act in connection with the elements and the moon: to sow seeds with the new or full moon, depending on what you are growing and the layout of vases along cardinal points. This will help awaken hidden memories, because it brings us back to where we came from.

The garden allows the witch to realize that everything she is learning she already knew. Even you know. Because your grand-mothers, great-grandmothers, and ancestors grew herbs and understood the natural world without having to study, through practice. By practicing gardening, both the witch and the garden can grow and be transformed. Having a garden means recognizing that humans and the earth are a single system, a body full of life, connected to plants, animals, and the whole cosmos. All you have to do is remember.

WHOM WE WILL FIND ON THE PATH OF GREEN MAGIC

✦ ✦ ✦

The path of green magic is by its nature a lonely path. The practice of a green witch tends to be an individual practice that stands in harmony with and conveys empathy toward the nature that surrounds her. The first meaning of the green path is being sensitive and open to the natural world. It means recognizing the footprints of deer in the woods, respecting the stinging nettle, observing the spiral of a sprouting fern, enjoying the sunlight filtering through the leaves of the oak, and embracing the stillness of winter under the snow.

It's important to use the word *path* when we refer to green magic. This practice is immersive, total. A green witch does not act outside of the ordinary (for example, in a magic ritual) but rather lives her daily life as a source of spiritual and sacred energy. A green witch walks the path of magic and makes it individual and specific. That's why each green witch has her own vision and particular way of coming into contact with the magic of everything: herbs, trees, animals, forests, waves, shells, the moon.

Along this path, we will meet three types of witches, who share a daily and solitary practice rooted in popular traditions: the green witch, often called the natural witch; the kitchen witch; and the hedge witch. Let's get to know them better.

THE GREEN WITCH

+ ✦ +

A green witch does not necessarily live on the edge of the woods, surrounded by medicinal herbs, ferns, and owls. There are also green witches who live in the city and grow plants on their windowsill. They feel and live their relationship to nature in a special way, and this contact can exist in any environment.

The green witch lives and practices her spirituality *through* the natural world. For her the woods are a sacred place, plants know how to listen, and animals are travel companions. The green witch is closely connected to the earth element, and her magic is found in the manifestation of natural forces and in forms of healing connected to the elements. To her, magic and life are interconnected, because life itself is a magical experience.

The green witch welcomes you with a vigorous and fragrant infusion of nettle and rose petals, still steaming from the stove. Her plants—mint, basil, and sage for purifying—grow in little greenhouses. She welcomes you with care. She is a manifestation of Mother Earth, she who nurtures, cares, and observes. She practices with herbs, plants, and remedies and surely has volumes upon volumes of plant books on her bookshelves.

THE KITCHEN WITCH

+ ✦ +

When my mother would cut white onions, I would think about how they looked like half-moons; when my grandmother cooks tomato sauce, she asks me to bring her basil leaves. And when I walk toward the kitchen, with the memory of my mother and the smell of herbs on her hands, I think about how the kitchen is a truly magical place of tradition and creation. This is the magic of the kitchen witch. She works with ordinary tools and understands the sacred aspects of everyday life as she prepares food and eats it.

For her, the practices of the kitchen are spells: kneading bread with intention and watching it rise along with her desires, stirring the ingredients of a cake clockwise to bring joy and love to the life of whoever eats it, choosing vegetables to make a comforting soup, and recognizing that the magic cauldron is not so different from the pot bubbling on the stove. The kitchen witch works intuitively, adding a pinch of salt or lowering the heat, tasting and listening and improvising according to the nourishing energy of food. She is a witch of the earth element. For her, food, a gift from Mother Earth, is sacred. Our body is a temple that we must take care of through what we eat, and she knows how to cook that food well.

She knows that the act of cooking reveals our divine nature. She follows the smell of berries and citrus, freshly baked bread, good food. You will find her waiting for you in the kitchen behind a mug of steaming chocolate, her dark eyes staring back at you.

THE HEDGE
WITCH

+ ✦ +

E ver since ancient times, there has been an old woman living on the edge of the woods. Whether she's near a forest, at the end of a village road, or beyond the last hedge, this figure lives in our collective imagination. The hedge witch lives on the edge. She collects herbs; she heals and cures. She is a shaman. *She knows.* Those who live on the edge know how to cross worlds, travel between this world and that of dreams, bringing symbolic messages and healing. The hedge witch is a medicine woman, an herbalist, a healer. Those who live on the edge know how to cut through the hedge that divides the known from the unknown, the village from the woods, the cultivated from the wild.

The hedge witch knows that whatever limits and protects is necessary. There are often foxes, mice, and other small animals that shelter in hedges. Often, hedges are magical, containing healing plants like hawthorn or laurel. For the hedge witch, solitude is very important, and she knows that even when she is by herself, she is not truly alone, because she feels a deep connection with nature around her, which makes her feel renewed. In the absence of rituals and specific traditions, she acts by following the influences of the place where she lives.

The hedge witch knows the power of fables and preserves popular knowledge. In the evening, next to the fire, she can tell your story too. Listen to her carefully when you meet her.

A QUICK DETOUR: POISONOUS PLANTS

✦ ✦ ✦

The word "poison," just like the word "witch," has always had an ambiguous meaning. The Latin word for "witch" is *strix*, meaning owl, which is a symbol of wisdom and foresight as well as a notion of darkness and fear. Likewise, poison has many different and opposing meanings. The Latin word *venenum* means poison but also potion, like the Greek word *pharmakon*, which means medicine, spell, and poison.

As Paracelsus said, "All things are poison . . . the dosage alone makes it so a thing is not a poison." Those who choose to walk the green path will surely come across poisonous plants. Upon closer inspection, these plants simply have more concentrated doses of toxins and other active ingredients than do healing plants. Poisonous plants are often lunar plants with a particular shape, color, and structure. We will get to know some up close in order to come into contact with their strong energy and message. But contact with poisonous plants must always be expressed without consuming them. Many can lead to death if even a small amount is ingested.

Poisonous plants are interesting because they speak directly to the dark, hidden dream side of every person. Knowing only the solar medicinal plants and ignoring poisonous ones will only disrupt balance. We may move closer to poisonous plants in order to become in tune with the more hidden side of ourselves, the side we ignore or often try to suffocate. So, with the help of these plants, we can start working on the very important act of self-awareness: integrating the darker sides, learning to give them a voice. The message of poisonous plants is largely directed at the free and wild parts of ourselves.

CHAPTER 1

THE TOOLS
OF A WITCH

MANY OF THE TOOLS OF THE GREEN
WITCH ARE USED DAILY, BUT SHE USES
THEM FOR MAGICAL TASKS, TO COME
INTO CONTACT WITH THE EARTH,
WITH WHAT NOURISHES US
AND MAKES US THRIVE.

⚡ ⚡ ⚡

Let's enter the green witch's cupboard: We will find mortars, broomsticks, and dried herbs. Let's take a look in the pantry of the kitchen witch, where we will smell her spices and find her magic wand. Let's tiptoe through the wild garden of the hedge witch, where there are nasturtium vines and bags of magic seeds.

EVERY WITCH
HAS HER TOOLS

⚡ ⚡ ⚡

When we think about a witch, we imagine her in a cave surrounded by vials of potions, alembics, hanging plants drying upside down, and boiling cauldrons. She is there, intent on the task before her, trusty magic wand in hand and ready to direct her energy and desires.

It's true that a wand helps one focus on magical acts, just like a cauldron can be indispensable for liquefying perfumed oils and beeswax as well as creating healing unguents. But a witch knows that her main tool is herself: her body, intentions, intuition, will. One's body responds to the elements; it represents them. Bones are connected to the earth. They provide structure and hold our story, being related to our ancestors and what remains of us. Fire is in the blood, which represents life, passion, activity. It is red thanks to iron, represented by Mars, the planet and god. The light, communicative air enters us through our breath, which is life-giving and spiritual; the root of this word is *spiritus*, which in Latin means air, breath, and vital force. Water, the element we are largely composed of,

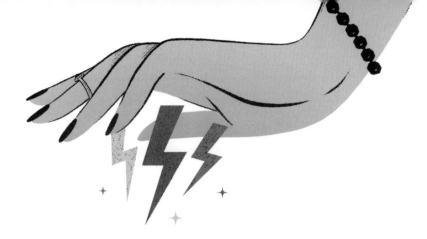

eventually turns into joy, pain, emotion through our tears. Finally, the fifth element, ether, which is tied to intuition, bonds the other elements, harmonizing them and allowing a witch to do magic.

A witch's tools are therefore very personal. There are no specific tools, especially along the green path, which, as we have seen, is very intuitive. According to Wiccan tradition, the basic tools of a witch refer to the four elements. The magic wand is associated with fire, moving and focusing energy. The goblet, the water tool, holds the water of the moon, infuses magical teas, and is used for divinatory practices. The athame, a witch's knife, is tied to the air; it is used to open and close the magic circle and to ban and punish. The pentagram, often drawn or inscribed on a dish or created by laying stones, herbs, or talismans to be filled with energy, is used to offer nourishment to the earth. For some, the athame and wand are associated with fire and air, respectively, but I believe the opposite is true.

With this foundation, we may begin to observe how these tools can be substituted for each other, combined, and interpreted personally. Magical acts are individual actions. Choosing our tools carefully, adapting them to our practice, is a way to come into contact with our power and with the possibility of manifesting our dreams. These tools are necessary in order to make what we imagine visible.

THE CUPBOARD OF
THE GREEN WITCH

Every green witch has her special cupboard. Inside are jars of herbs, several mortars, syrups, and flower petals. Every green witch has her favorite tools, which can be used to come into contact with nature, collect herbs, and transform them. Most importantly, she uses her hands to handle the plants and harvest from them. She also uses her senses to understand things, her sense of touch being extremely useful for perceiving the message of plants and their energy.

1. SMUDGE STICK

MADE WITH SAGE, CEDAR, ROSEMARY, AND OTHER PURIFYING HERBS TO CLEAR THE AIR OF NEGATIVE ENERGY

2. MORTAR

NECESSARY FOR PREPARING POWDERS, INCENSE, AND FLOWER BLENDS

4. JARS OF HERBS

TO STORE LEAVES, FLOWERS, ROOTS, AND SEEDS

3. SCISSORS

NEVER GO OUTSIDE WITHOUT SCISSORS. YOU MIGHT COME ACROSS HERBS YOU WISH TO COLLECT!

5. SCALE

TO WEIGH INGREDIENTS FOR SALVES
AND POTIONS

6. HERBAL PILLOW

FOR PROPHETIC DREAMS

7. ALEMBIC

TO MAKE ALCHEMICAL
BREWS AND PERFUMES

8. HERBAL INKS

FOR WRITING
MAGICAL LABELS

9. BUNCHES OF HERBS

HERBS COLLECTED UNDER
THE MOONLIGHT
OR AT DAWN
AND HUNG TO DRY

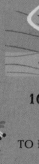

10. BOTTLED DEW

TO ENHANCE ELIXIRS
AND POTIONS

THE PANTRY OF THE KITCHEN WITCH

The kitchen is this witch's sacred space, the place where all the elements meet to create alchemy. The kitchen witch is the intimate fire that we gather around in the evening to share what happened that day and what we wish for tomorrow. Her kitchen is a room of senses that listens and nourishes and has a remedy for every pain. Her altar is found between the cauldron bubbling on the stove and the smell of rosemary hanging from a blue string. These are only a few of her tools!

2. WOODEN SPOON

OFTEN DECORATED WITH SYMBOLS OR RUNES, IT INSTILLS THE INTENTION OF OUR DESIRES

1. CAULDRON

THE ROUNDED POT BUBBLING ON THE WOOD-FIRE STOVE

4. JARS OF SEEDS

TO PUT IN SALADS THAT SUMMON ABUNDANCE

3. BUTCHER BLOCK

FOR KNEADING MAGIC BREAD AND LETTING IT RISE

6. MAGICAL PRESERVES

ENHANCED WITH FLOWER BUDS,
PETALS, AND HONEY

5. COLORFUL SPICES

CHOSEN WITH CARE

7. RED TEAPOT

AND INFINITE COMFORTING TEAS
READY TO DRINK

8. HERBS

SAVED FROM A SUPERMARKET AND LEFT
TO GROW ON THE WINDOWSILL

9. MOON-SHAPED
COOKIES

FOR EVERY LUNAR
PHASE

10. MAGICAL RECIPE BOOK

WITH RECIPES, EXPERIMENTS,
AND MAGICAL PRACTICES

THE SHED
OF THE HEDGE WITCH

There, next to her home at the edge of the woods, is the hedge witch's shed. It's where she keeps the tools needed for her trips, whether she's traveling into the woods or into other dimensions. A few foxes have built their den there, and, just outside, cats keep watch at the doorstep. Inside there are seeds for the garden, numerous vases, some galvanized watering cans, a glass shard that hangs from the ceiling casting rainbows, and many more items . . . .

1. SORGHUM BROOMSTICK

TO CLEANSE THE HOUSE
OF NEGATIVE INFLUENCES

2. OLD BOOTS

TO WALK THROUGH THE GARDEN
OR UNDER THE RAIN

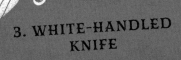

3. WHITE-HANDLED KNIFE

TO COLLECT HEALING HERBS

4. FRESHLY SPROUTED MANDRAKES

TO BE PLANTED
IN THE MAGIC GARDEN

5. SORB TREE FRUITS

TIED TOGETHER TO DRIVE AWAY
UNWANTED SPIRITS

6. TWO ENAMELED MUGS

TO SHARE INFUSIONS
WITH FRIENDS

7. COMFORTABLE CUSHION

TO HOST ANIMAL FRIENDS
IN THE WINTER

8. SLEEPING BAG

TO SLEEP UNDER
THE STARS

9. LANTERN

FOR WALKS IN THE WOODS
AT NIGHT

10. RARE AND PRECIOUS SEEDS

TO GROW MAGICAL
INGREDIENTS

Chapter 2

YOUR HOME
IS YOUR TEMPLE

SOMEONE'S HOME SAYS A LOT ABOUT A PERSON. I LIKE TO IMAGINE THE PERSON WHO LIVES BEHIND THE DOORS OF ANY HOME I GO INTO.

◆ ◆ ◆

The place where we live is an extension of ourselves, permeated by our energy, a safe and comfortable place to recharge and share a sense of well-being with those we love. A green witch has a close relationship with the environment she lives in, whether it's near a chestnut grove, in the mountains, or simply next to a public park in the city. Anywhere you live can become sacred through care and attention. Taking care of the place where we live means loving ourselves.

PURIFYING YOUR HOME WITH HERBS

◆ ◆ ◆

Our home can be a magical tool that helps increase our well-being, recharge our energy, and keep us rooted. One way to take care of our home is by purifying it—something we can also do to other magical tools. But what does it mean to *purify your home?*

Purification for a green witch is magical cleaning. Certain practices are used to clear stagnant energy that can burden the environment we live in.

The simplest purification technique is cleaning. A bright and beautiful home without heaps of dust behind the door or under the bed favors a light and vibrant flow of energy. We can use these herbs to enhance our cleaning and make them magical:

- **MUGWORT:** a lunar plant of protection. The most common variety (*Artemisia vulgaris*) is used as an amulet for travel. You can make an infusion of its leaves mixed with water for cleaning.

- **SAGE:** the most common plant used to purify spaces is sacred sage (*Salvia apiana*). It originates in Central America and is used by native people in purification ceremonies. Otherwise, use common sage (*Salvia officinalis*), found in smudge sticks, which will be discussed on page 38.

- **PALO SANTO:** the special wood of a tropical tree called *Bursera graveolens*. It soaks up the fragrant sap only after it has died and after remaining underground for many years. When lit, if the flame is blown out, it continues to burn slowly, spreading the smell of balsam throughout the space and cleaning its energy.

MAGICAL PRACTICES OF PURIFICATION

◆ ◆ ◆

SMUDGE STICK

To best use purifying herbs, you can create a smudge stick, a bundle of dried herbs tied together and lit as if it were an incense stick. To make a smudge stick, collect some fresh herbs with purifying and protective properties, like mugwort, sage, rosemary, cedar, Saint-John's-wort, or lavender. Tie them together with a natural fiber string (twine or cotton), folding up the ends of the plants and creating a small wand. Let it dry in a cool, dry place. Once the herbs are dry, light it; then put out the flame and let the smoke filter through each room. Do this with the windows open so that the smoke shoos away the stagnant energy of your home.

WITCH'S BROOM

For this practice, use a broom made of natural materials; avoid plastic and nylon. Open all the windows, and wave the broom as if you were sweeping away the still and stagnant air without touching the floor. Do so in a counterclockwise motion, which is traditionally associated with the clearing of negative energy. Once you have finished, say out loud, "This room is clean, and the light shines in every corner."

COARSE SALT

Salt absorbs and cleans. Put some coarse salt in a small dish in each room; in a corner is best. You can also put a few grains on windowsills and in the doorway. As you do so, ask the earth to keep your space clean. Change the salt regularly until you feel the environment is light and luminous.

ENCHANTED BELLS, CANDLES, AND INCENSE

◆ ◆ ◆

Sounds help bring new vibrations to your home. Even the music you love can realign your space with the air element. It's pure vibration: Just think about how much music affects your emotions and memories.

Hang a few bells on the window, and let the wind move them to bring enchanted sounds to your home. If you would like to add more powerful magic, hang small glass prisms next to the bells. When the sun hits them, your home will have thousands of dancing rainbows!

Incense is also connected to the air element. You can make purifying incense yourself by mixing the following:

- one part **granulated incense**
- one part **copal resin**
- one part **dried lemon zest**
- one part **dried lavender flowers**
- one part **dried sage flowers and leaves**

Put a pinch of the mixture on a lit piece of charcoal on a heat-resistant incense holder, and let the fragrant smoke spread throughout your home. Always remember to air out the space after.

Coarse salt is connected to the earth element, bells and incense are linked to the air element, and fire is added by lighting some candles. The flame improves the atmosphere, offers enchanting light, and favors relaxation and well-being.

To maximize your use of candles, add scented oils with the smells of plants and protective herbs. You can mix the following oils:

- 3.4 fluid ounces (100 ml) of **sweet almond oil**
- 10 drops of **thyme oil**
- 15 drops of **lavender oil**
- 10 drops of **lemon oil**
- 5 drops of **cedar oil**

Together they will spread magic!

CHAPTER 3

ENTER YOUR SECRET GARDEN

IT DOESN'T HAVE TO BE LARGE, OR EVEN YOURS. YOUR SECRET GARDEN IS SIMPLY THE PLACE WHERE YOU FEEL IN TOUCH WITH NATURE.

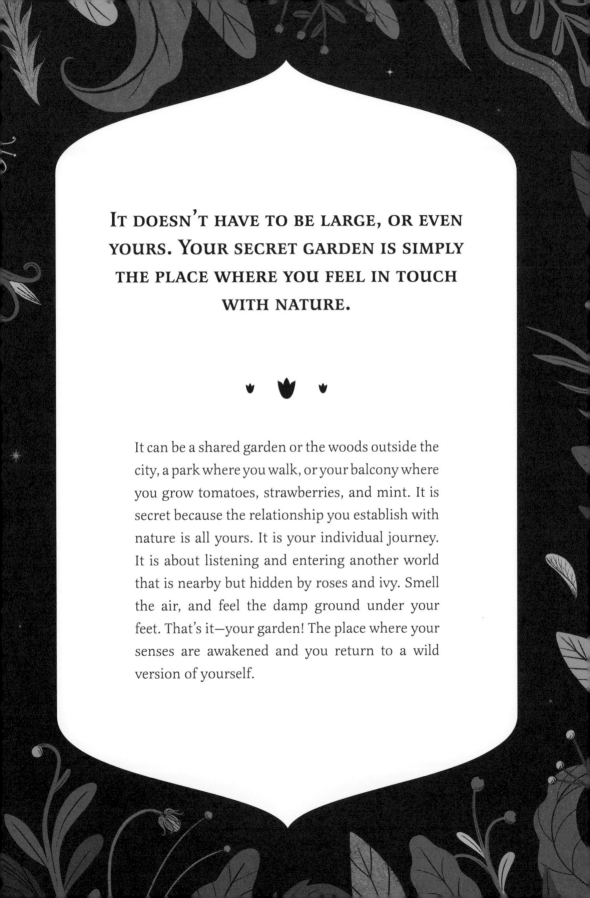

It can be a shared garden or the woods outside the city, a park where you walk, or your balcony where you grow tomatoes, strawberries, and mint. It is secret because the relationship you establish with nature is all yours. It is your individual journey. It is about listening and entering another world that is nearby but hidden by roses and ivy. Smell the air, and feel the damp ground under your feet. That's it—your garden! The place where your senses are awakened and you return to a wild version of yourself.

PREPARING
A SACRED SPACE
OUTDOORS

🌷

In order to rediscover the sacredness and simplicity of green magic in us, we can create a sacred space outdoors. With the same care and attention we gave our home, we can bring order, good vibrations, and magic outdoors.

Enter your secret garden and find a comfortable spot. Sense the natural elements in the environment: air, water, earth, and fire. Try to create a bond with them. Feel the wind, plunge your hands in the water of the fountain, draw a line in the earth, caress the leaves, be warmed by the sun . . . . Through these gestures, you can become part of your sacred space and help in its creation. It's simple: You just have to listen. At this point, observe what plants grow in this space, whether it's a tree or a potted basil plant. If you do not recognize all of them, take a photo and search on the internet or ask an herbalist. Find out the plant's name and properties, as if you were making a new friend. Get to know the plants that live there. You can do the same thing with the wild animals who leave their tracks and with rocks found in the area.

You might want to mark the bounds of your sacred space. You can draw a circle on the ground, delineate it with special grass, or use stones, sticks, rocks, petals, or leaves to create a plant mandala that will be carried away by the wind. You could even just imagine a sphere of light that encompasses this space, above and below the ground.

Once you have established contact with whomever lives in your sacred space and made the limits of your space visible, find a way to inaugurate it. You can invent how. It could be a simple phrase, a song, a whisper.

And that's it. The magic is done. This is your sacred space.

ALTARS UNDER THE MOON

*A*fter you have met the beings that populate your space, take something that recalls each natural element to create your altar.

Feathers, bells, winged seeds, and light strings are tied to the air element. You can use pebbles, small pearls, polished glass shards, dewdrops, and river water for the water element. For the earth element, you can choose between acorns, moss, chestnuts, autumnal leaves, bark, and various seeds. And finally there are red strings, yellow leaves and flowers, golden leaflets, red stones, colored seeds, or a small candle, which represent fire. (The candle must be watched carefully when lit; *never* leave a candle lit when you are gone.) Let your intuition freely choose what works best for you.

You can put everything in a small bag or box that you then carry with you to your sacred space. Identify the cardinal points, and place your chosen objects in this format:

East: **Air**   West: **Water**   North: **Earth**   South: **Fire**

Now your altar is ready. You can use it to meditate, recharge stones or talismans, or celebrate an event. Remember that the altar is a magical expression of whoever created it and is mainly used to connect us with the everyday divine aspect of ourselves. This altar makes the beauty of connections between great and small more visible. These are the connections between what is around us and what lives inside us.

ROOTING PRACTICES

❦

There are some basic practices of rooting and centering. I would like to suggest those that I developed through observation and the relationship I have with plants, particularly their roots.

Let's look at what roots are symbolically.

- The **main root,** which is partially developed, makes me think of the plant's ability to be what it is, to root its personality in the ground. The main root is also a symbol of will. It is the first root to sprout from the seed, saying, *Hey, here I am. I want to be!* Sometimes plants with a large main root are easily uprooted. This could be a symptom of poor attachment to things or matters in life.

  For you, the main root could be the ability to enter into a deeper understanding of things. What pushes you to this deeper understanding? What would you like to explore in more detail?

- **Secondary roots** are the parts that explore the territory, going in search of water and nutrients, meeting other roots. They are the social part of the plant, and it is interesting to observe how they develop, whether they go in search of nearby plants or not. They can tell you much about the character of a plant.

How do you take care of your secondary roots? How are your relationships? Sometimes we find ourselves in difficulty; important relationships can end, and we fear we will no longer receive the nutrients we need for happiness. However, sometimes we just need to change direction, observe those around us, and extend our secondary roots to shake hands, create bonds, and forge love.

- Finally, there are **rhizome roots,** which are modified roots. Think of a potato. It distributes energy and nutrients for the plant. Rhizomes are a safe space, a home, the place where you will always find what you want, the place that nurtures you. My rhizomes are tearooms, bookstores, and my grandmother's kitchen.

Think of where you can always find those things that make you feel good. Search for your refuge, celebrate it, make a nest, and listen to your needs. Find your perfect place—your rhizome!

CENTERING PRACTICES

♥ ♥ ♥

Centering is a practice that allows us to be in the here and now. It is a moment in which we are aware of who we are and what we are doing, being interconnected with people, plants, and animals.

Here are a few simple practices of centering.

- **_Visualization_**. Find a moment just for you, even just ten minutes. Sit in a comfortable position, close your eyes, and listen to your breath. Listen to the air entering and leaving your lungs, entering and leaving. Focus on your breath and nothing else. Relax and imagine that roots are sprouting from the bottom of your spine. Your roots can be whatever you imagine them to be: nodal, powerful, green, fresh, or even silver. Imagine that your roots are penetrating the earth—that it is cool, soft, and dark. You see a light rise from your roots and reach your spine before leaving through the top of your head and then falling back down to earth. Sit in this circle of light in which you give energy to the earth and receive it through your roots. Return to your breath. When you feel like it, reopen your eyes.

- **_Harvest_**. Go to a garden in a park or the countryside and pick a bouquet of flowers. Focus on the sounds you hear, the shapes of the flowers, the smell of the earth. Stay connected to the earth, then bring your flowers to your altar or put them in a vase at home. They will remind you that you, too, are a flower.

- **Barefoot**. Whenever you get the chance, take off your shoes and socks and walk barefoot in the grass in a safe place. Feel the earth supporting you. Feel how soft or hard, wet or dry, it is. Pay attention to the grass; feel its touch on the bottom of your foot. Hold on to this feeling even when you are wearing shoes.

- **A slow moment**. Make a cup of tea. Light some incense or palo santo or your favorite candle. Let your mind go, and breathe deeply. Stay there, in that moment, with everything it consists of.

CHAPTER 4

THE FOUR NATURAL ELEMENTS AND THEIR PLANTS

COMING INTO CONTACT WITH NATURAL
MAGIC MEANS COMPREHENSIVELY
KNOWING THE FOUR ELEMENTS—AIR,
WATER, EARTH, AND FIRE—AND THE
PLANTS THAT CARRY THEIR MESSAGES.

In this chapter, we will get to know some plants
that represent each element and learn about
them so that we can collect and become closer
to them. Every plant has its own voice. Here you
will discover their message.

AIR PLANTS

✦

YARROW

DANDELION

SPEARMINT

The plants tied to the air element usually have a balsamic scent, like mint and lavender. Just like air, they love to communicate. They are light and like to extend themselves with intense smells through which they manifest their presence from afar. Air plants are connected to Mercury, the god of communication and speed, as well as Jupiter, the god of generation and regulation. Often they have hollow stems and light seeds, like fennel and cumin, that are blown away by the wind.

YARROW

Achillea millefolium

Yarrow grows in fields from the beginning of summer. You can recognize it from its small white or pink flowers that blossom in tall flower heads. Its name comes from Achilles, who cured his friend Patroclus with the plant.

Yarrow is an air plant, representing the element's lightness and strength. Yarrow waves lightly in the summer breeze and spreads its unmistakable herbaceous, woodsy scent, which smells of summer in the mountains. At the same time, it grows slowly and strongly, day by day, all season long. Once picked, it dries perfectly.

Yarrow has many properties. It helps wounds heal, improves blood flow, helps with menstrual cramps, and is a digestive, diuretic, and depurative for the liver. It can help with headaches, fever, colds, and general discomfort. Like Achilles, who saved his friend, yarrow repairs and soothes and is a warrior plant that acts with determination and consistency. It is also good at healing the wounds of love. It carries out its work along scars, keeping out what must stay out and in what must stay in. It teaches you to take care of your sacred space, to protect it and protect yourself.

Its subtle message is: *Protect your space so that it may flower fully.*

DANDELION

Taraxacum officinale

Dandelion is marked by the air element in many of its parts, starting with the leaves, which have a toothed pattern that varies from plant to plant. I have always thought that the variety seen in its leaves is indicative of the versatility and creativity of the dandelion. The seeds have characteristic tufts called pappi that together form the well-known seed head you can blow. The seeds are transported through the air to discover new places.

Dandelion is also a symbol of perseverance. How many times have you seen it pop up in the middle of a city between the cracks of some steps or the asphalt of a road? Dandelion is tenacious, exuberant, and sunny, given its marking by Jupiter. The planet and the element have left these signs and symbols, which help guide one in using it.

Dandelion is very useful in purifying, draining, and stimulating the liver by cleaning out toxins. It is a spring plant that helps us detox our body of the dregs of winter and prepare it for the hottest season. Every part of the dandelion is used. The root, when dried and cleaned, is great for herbal teas with depurative and draining effects. The young leaves are great in salads, and, when mature, they can be sautéed with garlic and hot pepper. The flowers can be pickled like capers. They are also used to make magic honey, a syrup of sugar and petals.

Its subtle message is: *Have faith, and do not fear.*

SPEARMINT

Mentha x *piperita*

Mentha is a genus that comprises many species. My favorite is spearmint. I keep some next to the door of my house. It's been there since my grandfather planted it. Mint is an air plant and is very communicative. The first thing you notice is its scent! The essential oils in its leaves are fresh and unmistakable. Spearmint can adapt to the needs of the moment. It is both a stimulant and relaxant, digestive and appetite-inducing, and so on. It is an amphoteric herb, which means it acts in the body according to what's needed. This is also a very air-like quality—adaptability, the ability to use intuition, a mercurial and changing liveliness. Like the messenger Mercury, mint is also listening and responding accordingly.

Spearmint is very active in the digestive and respiratory systems, places in our bodies where important exchanges take place. We can use mint to make teas for coughs, colds, and the inflammation of airways, inhaling its steam to fight bronchitis and asthma. It is a strong painkiller. Just a few drops in some almond oil rubbed on your temples can subdue a headache.

Spearmint clears the mind, activates your inner vision, and improves focus and intention. It brings freshness and levity and knows how to dive deep while remaining easy.

Its subtle message is: *Keep your thoughts light, and you will see more clearly.*

FIRE PLANTS

>>•<<

SAINT-JOHN'S-WORT

MARIGOLD

NETTLE

Plants that sting or are spicy and hot are fire plants. They carry the signs of Mars and the sun. They act on the skin, like with burns and rashes, or on the blood and circulation. They are usually warm colors: yellow, orange, and red.

SAINT-JOHN'S-WORT

Hypericum perforatum

Saint-John's-wort is one of the greatest sun plants. It traps the light in its five petals that form a star, and every part of the plant contains a red oil that can stain your hands when you pick it. Saint-John's-wort recalls summer, sunlight, and warmth. It is known to ward off evil spirits. Hanging a small bunch of the flower at the door of your home will protect it from negative influences, but just encountering this truly magical plant will show you its luminous energy.

Phytotherapy is also a result of its being marked by fire and sun. It is the main plant used for sunburn, burns, and rashes. But it is also photosensitive. If you put some oil on your skin before going into the sun, it could cause itching and redness. Ingesting it is also a matter of light; it inhibits serotonin reuptake and therefore fights depression, a dark side of the soul.

The balsamic moment of the plant—when its main ingredients are most present—falls around the summer solstice and the night of Saint John's feast day, June 24. This is when it should be picked to make its oil. The flowers are left to macerate in olive oil in a jar covered by cloth in the sun for forty days. Then the oil is filtered. It is red like blood and recalls the plant's vital properties. It is effective against any discomfort related to the fire element.

Its subtle message is: *Do not fear; the light shines where the shadow is darkest.*

MARIGOLD

Calendula officinalis

The fire of the marigold is different from that of Saint-John's-wort. It is an intimate, gentle fire. It has a moon side hidden inside it. Marigold flowers are an intense orange and are warm and cheerful like the flower itself, which is small and herbaceous with resinous leaves. When you pick its flower heads, your fingers become sticky and smell good. The intimate, female part of the marigold lies in its delicate, light, half-moon–shaped seed. The marigold has a deep relationship with the environment. It has hygroscopic properties, and its flowers close up when a storm is arriving. If it lives in temperate climates, it flowers every month, giving it its scientific name, calendula, from the Latin *calendae,* referring to the first day of the month in ancient Rome.

Marigold is also effective against inflammation and burns, but it is gentler and more soothing. It is therefore recommended for the delicate skin of babies. Its internal use proves that it is a lunar plant since it regulates menstrual flow and is helpful with pain, amenorrhea, or irregularity.

When dried, the petals retain their intense color and are added to teas even just for looks. The marigold's light is destined to remain bright. According to legend, if a girl were to walk barefoot on marigolds, she would be able to understand the language of birds. I like to think that this speaks to the hidden uniqueness of this plant and that it has extraordinary power to offer women.

Its subtle message is: *Your light is stronger if it shines alongside others.*

NETTLE

Urtica dioica

*L*ike yarrow, nettle is a warrior plant with a martial sign. It has burning leaves rich in formic acid as well as an ability to regenerate blood. It is by all means a fire plant, but less solar and more earthly: the green fire of spring, the strength of the sprout that breaks through the dirt in March, the month dedicated to Mars and the sign Aries. Nettle defends its territory and imposes its presence. You only need to brush past it to realize it is there! But if you try to establish a relationship with it, you will find it to be generous and nourishing. You can make an excellent fertilizer for your garden with nettles so that all your plants can benefit from the micronutrients of its leaves. It is also great for us, especially when we are tired, weary, and lacking energy. Nettle favors the formation of ferritin, a fundamental enzyme for absorbing iron, and therefore helps with anemia and persistent lethargy. Its high chlorophyll content can regenerate hemoglobin, purifying and renewing the blood.

Nettle teaches individuality and calls us to pay attention. It is important to recognize the talents and resources of everyone without making rushed conclusions. It also teaches us that although something might sting at first, it can become an excellent ally. You just need to know how to take it.

Its subtle message is: *Pay attention and be sure to understand the special side of things.*

WATER PLANTS

MUGWORT

ALOE

GREATER BURDOCK

Water plants are lunar plants rich in mucilage with strange or very small flowers that are often light-colored. They love shady or damp places. They are delicate, elegant, eccentric plants.

MUGWORT

Artemisia vulgaris

Mugwort is one of the plants most closely connected to the moon. Its double-faced leaves prove this. They are dark green on the front and bright silver on the back. Mugwort is connected to the untamed spirit of the goddess Artemis and her wild female power. It is strengthening for the female. It is considered sacred by Native Americans and is used in fumigations that clean the environment and protect against negative influences.

Mugwort lives on the threshold, is associated with dreams, and is used to travel safely between the dream world and the real world. It is also connected with the visionary power of water: It expands our ability to see even where we might think there is nothing to see. Adding a few leaves to your evening tea or putting them under your pillow will make your dreams clearer.

When ingested, mugwort has digestive and tonic properties. Its leaves contain calcium and help strengthen bones. You can make a special vinegar from its leaves by letting them steep in wine vinegar for at least two weeks. It is great for integrating calcium, which is an important ally in menopause.

It is a protective plant that women in Japan use to clean the doorways of homes so that demons stay out. In Europe, it is traditionally considered protective for travel.

Its subtle message is: *Trust your moon.*

ALOE

Aloe vera

*A*loe is an African plant but is commonly found in Europe as well. Its leaves form a rose shape, but there are also varieties that grow from a strong central stem. It is a very valuable plant connected to the water element, primarily for its plump leaves, which contain a watery gel with soothing, calming, and refreshing properties. Its water gives life despite the circumstances. Aloe has a lot to offer.

Aloe's properties are endless. The gel is used on the skin and hair to deeply hydrate, clean, improve oxygenation, and help exchange and purge toxins. It stimulates the defense mechanisms of the skin against aging and the development of free radicals. It protects and heals. Like Saint-John's-wort, aloe can be used to treat burns and rashes and prevent blistering. The power of this plant is regenerative, just like water in the desert. It hydrates, feeds, calms, and comforts.

The best way to use aloe gel is to harvest it yourself from the leaves—preferably one of the older ones. Once it is cut, you can get rid of the external part of the leaf with a knife and rub the gel directly on the skin.

Its subtle message is: *There is wealth where you least expect it; you just need to look.*

GREATER BURDOCK

Arctium lappa

Greater burdock is a plant of movement, which we can see from the structure of its fruits. They are hooked and get stuck on the clothes of anyone who brushes past them, off to explore the world. Greater burdock is tied to the water element because it can both fluidify liquids that are stagnant in our body and hydrate tissues. It helps bring balance to our organism. It is rich in mucilage and is refreshing and detoxing. It is particularly useful for the liver, helping drain it of toxins. It can also alleviate acne and alcohol intoxication, thanks to its purifying and calming properties.

Greater burdock aids people with tempers who are easily angered or heated. The most commonly used part of the plant is the root, which is eaten in Japan and used by Native Americans as food or medication for the skin. In Europe, its large leaves are traditionally used to soothe inflammation of the bronchi by applying it to the chest after it is oiled.

Greater burdock is a protective plant. The root can be burned in the four corners of your house to protect it. The flowers are a symbol of abundance, and the whole plant is connected to the bear. It is used if you want to connect with the animal as a guide. Its scientific name, *Arctium,* comes from the Greek word for bear.

Its subtle message is: *Transform your rage so that you may be free.*

LAND PLANTS

∙≫∙≻∙•∙≺∙≪∙

HORSETAIL

COMMON COMFREY

RIBWORT PLANTAIN

The plants connected to the earth element are essential plants that contain precious minerals and benefit the bones and body structure in general. Governed by Saturn, they strengthen, make stable, and create matter. They are resistant plants that are not very eye-catching. They often have origins that date back to ancient times.

HORSETAIL

Equisetum arvense

Horsetail is a unique plant. It reproduces not by seeds but by spores that are contained in a small, elongated cone called a strobilus, which appears at the beginning of spring at the top of a bare, whitish stem. Once it has reproduced, this stem disappears and the plant generates a sterile stem, the most recognizable part, which is used in herbalist shops. This part is green, slightly branched, and similar in structure to a spine. The plant is prehistoric, appearing around 350 million years ago, and has remained unaltered.

Horsetail is rich in minerals. Traces of gold have even been found in the plant. In cases of osteoporosis and menopause, it helps bring minerals to the bones. It is also diuretic. Horsetail helps eliminate liquids, while also reintegrating mineral salts. In fact, it is a plant that works with balance—both for its appearance and its therapeutic properties—and that's why it is connected to the earth element. It strengthens and supports structure. It can be used magically to carefully and precisely reinforce our boundaries. It reminds us that staying rigid can make us break and that durability comes from flexibility and adaptability, just like the spine supports the whole body but is also mobile and flexible.

Its subtle message is: *Remember to dance with the wind.*

COMMON COMFREY

Symphytum officinale

C ommon comfrey carries its message and function in its name: Its root contains allantoin, which helps consolidate tissues and makes our skin elastic. It also helps form the fibrocartilage callus. Applying a comfrey ointment on fractures can help with healing. Its scientific name offers a hint at its nature: *Symphytum* derives from the Greek word for "weld" or "unite." Common comfrey suggests that it is not possible to truly repair things alone but rather that it should be done with others. Its message tied to the earth element speaks of a common land full of encounters, exchanges, and belonging, uniting together, uniting forces, including, integrating, and leaving no one behind.

The leaves can be used to make an infused oil to cure eczema, varicose veins, and edemas. The water-based infusion of the plant is

used to fertilize gardens. But its main property is that it helps heal very rapidly. Therefore, it is recommended for disinfected wounds, to avoid infection from a healing that forms too quickly.

Common comfrey asks what needs to be healed. Once that's identified, take a moment to focus on the plan of action, then immerse yourself in it deeply.

Its subtle message is: *What if you found joy in the broken?*

RIBWORT PLANTAIN

Plantago major and *Plantago lanceolata*

It is said that travelers used to trust the fact that ribwort plantain grows near inhabited houses. When they saw it growing, it meant they were close to a town or shelter. It marks the space between inhabited and wild spaces. The land where it grows is both known and uncontaminated.

Some call it the herb of snakes, because it draws out toxins from our body. It's not a true antidote, but it definitely has draining and soothing properties. It is said that if you carry a piece of its root in your pocket, you will be protected from snakebites. It is rich in mucilage, and it can be used as a soothing poultice—either finely chopped fresh or chewed and applied—for cuts or insect bites. It can also be made into a syrup that is used for sore throats, colds, and respiratory inflammation. Ribwort plantain is an edible plant. The leaves are picked in spring when they are still tender, and they are blended with pine nuts and garlic to make a tasty pesto. A "wild" chef friend of mine said that its seeds smell like porcini mushrooms, and they can be lightly toasted in oil and then added to doughs and other mixes.

Ribwort plantain reminds us to return to the earth, into the earth, to make ourselves small, to look at things up close.

Its subtle message is: *Keep your heart wild, please.*

CHAPTER 5

POISONOUS PLANTS

(INCLUDING THOSE USED TO FLY ON A BROOM)

**POISONOUS PLANTS SPEAK DIRECTLY
TO OUR DARKER SIDE, THE SIDE THAT IS
CLOSELY RELATED TO DREAMS
AND THE IMAGINATION.**

☠ ☠ ☠

Their often extravagant shapes are a clear indication of their poisonous properties. Fairy tales often contain references to these unique plants, giving them the nickname "witches' plants." Poisonous plants are just as present as healing plants on the path of the green witch.

....

IMPORTANT: *These plants are poisonous and therefore should not be ingested in any form. Any relationship with these plants should be distant and should not include any consumption of the plants or derivatives of them.*

....

BELLADONNA

Atropa belladonna

☠ ☠ ☠

Belladonna is a nightshade plant in the Solanaceae family—a cousin to the tomato and eggplant. It grows in damp places, on the slopes of mountains and along rivers, in the countryside and along roads. It is a perennial plant with upright stems and rhizomatous roots, similar to a potato. The leaves are dark green, full, and oval. It gives off a bad odor, especially when the leaves are crumpled. The flowers are bell-shaped with purple or rose-colored corollas and dark yellow insides with red-violet veining. The fruits are shiny, black berries similar to cherries, but they are extremely poisonous. They mature between August and September.

Every part of belladonna is toxic. It contains hyoscyamine, scopolamine, and atropine, a toxin used in ophthalmology to dilate pupils. It is used in homeopathic medicine, but in all other cases ingestion is absolutely prohibited, as it could cause death.

Belladonna warns you of deceit in relationships. It reminds you that when love is unhealthy, it can paralyze and suffocate. Its ability to dilate the pupil is connected with what happens in love: the inability to focus and observe well, often because we don't listen to ourselves, losing sight of our needs and desires.

It is a plant that speaks to the heart and breath. It asks you if you have enough space in your relationship, or if you feel that some parts of you are suffocated, not free to express themselves. It pushes you to question yourself sincerely and carefully, rooting your strength in your heart and not losing yourself in love.

MANDRAKE

Mandragora officinarum

☠ ☠ ☠

Due to the anthropomorphic shape of its roots, mandrake has a long history of being associated with magic. Ever since antiquity, it's been recognized as having magical powers related to fertility and life, including aphrodisiac properties. In Hebrew, its name, *dudaim,* comes from the root *dod,* meaning love and loved. It is associated with seduction and occult powers, and according to some popular beliefs, it made witches invisible. Since it is connected to generative power, take necessary precautions and be very respectful when harvesting it. It is well-known that if the mandrake is poorly harvested, it will scream a cry so shrill that it can send you into madness. It is one of the plants that our ancestor witches used to attend sabbats. They would make an unguent from it—along with other hallucinogenic plants—that caused dizziness and the feeling of flying. Perhaps this is what the flying broomsticks really were!

Mandrake initially appears ordinary—with its elongated, wrinkly leaves and little violet flowers—but something special and unique is hiding underground. This, to me, gives a very clear message: We must unearth our talents and make our singular voice heard. It is a plant that brings euphoria and wild joy; it roots us in love, love for our talent or whatever makes us feel alive.

FLY AGARIC

Amanita muscaria

☠ ☠ ☠

Let me conclude my short aside on poisonous plants not with a plant but with a fungus. The fly agaric mushroom has a red cap with white dots and numerous gills on the hymenium, a meaty white stipe with a wide ring. Encountering a fly agaric in the woods, likely near a pine, oak, or spruce tree, makes you immediately feel like you are immersed in a fairy tale. The mushroom of the Caterpillar from *Alice in Wonderland* was a giant fly agaric! The history of this mushroom takes us way back in time. It was employed for centuries by shamans for curative and magical uses and to travel between worlds.

The fly agaric is poisonous and psychoactive: It causes hallucinations, tremors, a dream state, dizziness, and illusions of flying. One particular type of hallucination caused by consuming the fly agaric is called macropsia, in which the fungus alters vision and makes very small things look large. Its subtle message is tied to this: The fly agaric can help you assume a broader vision of things, looking at both the macrocosm and microcosm, when you have a limited view of a situation. It is connected to vision, broadens consciousness, and stimulates the imagination. It's no coincidence that Alice grows larger or smaller with the mushroom. Or is it just everything around her that changes size? Quite often the fly agaric says that the solution to things lies in a change of perspective.

HOW TO COME INTO SUBTLE CONTACT WITH PLANTS

☠ ☠ ☠

I f you ever venture through the woods near my house, you might find me sitting in front of a burdock plant, with my back leaned against an oak, or kneeling over small violet flowers that sprout up only in secret places.

It is possible to come into deeper contact with the plant world because plants communicate, speak, and move much more than they seem to. How might we come into contact with the plants we encounter along our green path? Start with these suggestions:

1. Carefully observe the plants that grow around your house. Even if you live in the city and there are only streets, alleys, and concrete around you, look closely and you will find some vagabond plants. These are spontaneous, resistant plants that safeguard beneficial properties and valuable stories. Once you have identified the plants that live near you, do some of your own research. Who are they? What are they called? What is their history? What are their phytotherapeutic properties? Get a nice notebook, and take notes about the information you find.

2. Get a sample of the plant and draw it. It doesn't matter if you don't know how to draw. Let yourself be inspired by the colors, shapes, and splendor of the plant, and put it in your album or notebook. Immerse yourself in its colors, the patterns of the leaves, the smells and textures.

3. Look for it in a calm place: the countryside, a city park, or your secret place. Now, sit near it, close your eyes, and listen. Try to identify with the plant. What does it see from its perspective? What sounds does it hear? What does it feel? Remain silent, waiting. Breathe deeply. And embrace its message. Then thank it and write about your experience in your notebook.

CHAPTER 6

THE GREEN WITCH'S LABORATORY

THE GREEN WITCH KNOWS HOW
TO MAKE UNGUENTS, HEALTHFUL OILS,
AND HERBAL TEAS WITH THE HERBS
SHE ENCOUNTERS ON HER PATH.

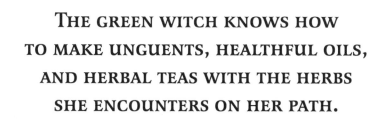

Whether you have a small kitchen; a room full of jars, flowers, and magical roots; or a real laboratory with many alembics, you can transform the herbs you harvest. Here, we will look at how to do so by taking a peek inside the heart of the witch's house, surrounded by a wood stove and bubbling potbellied cauldron; mandrake roots, dandelion flowers, and fragrant mint leaves; and the cat looking around furtively while pretending not to see.

GATHERING AND DRYING HERBS

• ◆ •

Before harvesting a plant, take the time to come into contact with its existence. Ask permission to take part of it, and say thanks after you have picked it. If you like, you can leave a little gift, like peat moss, a few nuts for animals, or a little bell for the fairies.

Gather only what you need, and no more than a third of the plant—and only where you can find many of the same plant.

All the recipes we will share can be made with the plants we have talked about so far—except, of course, the poisonous ones. If you aren't sure about a plant, don't pick it: instead, take some photos to show your local herbalist. NEVER pick plants you do not know.

Every plant has a peak moment, and each part should be harvested at a different time.

The roots should be harvested in autumn or the beginning of spring. They should be washed very well and cut up, then dried in a dehydrator at no higher than 95°F (35°C) or in a cool, dry place.

The leaves and stem should be picked when the plant is in full growth, but before flowering. They should not be washed but instead shaken to get rid of any possible insects. Then they should be tied up and hung to dry upside down in a cool, dry place. When they are ready, the leaves will crumble when touched.

Flowers should be picked when in full bloom, not wilted. They can be dried lying down in a cool, dry place away from sunlight. The flowers are also ready if they crumble when touched.

Finally, fruits should be collected when they are mature and dried like flowers.

All dried plants can be stored—best if kept for no longer than one year—in glass jars, sealed tight and kept away from sunlight and heat.

HERBAL TEAS
AND INFUSIONS

• ◆ •

The quickest way to use a plant you've gathered and dried is with a classic herbal tea. To make the perfect herbal tea, find some time to dedicate to it. The ritual aspect is a fundamental part. Choose your mug, fill up your teapot, light the flame, and let your mind wander. You can infuse the plants with intention. Place the herbs—one or two spoonfuls per cup—in a teapot or covered container so that you prevent the essential oils from evaporating. Once the water boils, turn off the flame and pour some of the water on the herbs.

Let it steep for five to fifteen minutes. Then filter it and enjoy, as you continue to think about your intention. You can give the herbs to the earth, put them in the compost, or use them in a pot as fertilizer for a plant.

For a sun-filled tea that's energizing, bright, and glowing, you can put the herbs in a clear-glass cup and fill it with lukewarm water. Put the cup in the sunlight for a few hours. The rays will warm your infusion. Filter and enjoy, feeling the harmony you've created with the message of the sun. You can also make a lunar tea with subtle properties that increase intuition as well as the ability to listen to your dreams and decode symbols. Choose the herbs you feel are closest to the moon's energy, and put them in a glass cup. Fill with lukewarm water and place in the light of the moon for the night. In the morning, filter and enjoy this light infusion and the lunar power it has absorbed.

TINCTURES

• ◆ •

In the green witch's laboratory, as well as in your kitchen, you can make tinctures, which are more concentrated herbal mixtures used for general well-being and to fight specific ailments. Let's take a look at how they are made.

Solvents
Many tinctures are made with alcohol, but they can also be made with unpasteurized cider vinegar. The solution will be less intense but more versatile.

Alcoholic solvent
For effective homemade preparations, you only need a solution of 40–50% alcohol and 50–60% water. Hard liquors like vodka already have this level proof (45–60%), and they can easily be used as solvents for tinctures.

How to make a tincture
1. Usually, 0.7 ounces (20 g) of dry plant per 3.4 fluid ounces (100 ml) of solvent are used. Break up your herbs into tiny pieces. If fresh, let them dry for a few hours.
2. Put them in a jar that can be closed hermetically. Cover the herbs with an alcoholic solution, then seal the jar.
3. Put the jar in a warm place away from the sun, and let it steep for at least four weeks.
4. If after a few days the herbs are floating, add some more alcohol so that it covers them by 1.2–1.6 inches (3–4 cm).
5. Filter the liquid and store in a dark glass bottle in a cool place. The tincture can be stored for up to two years.
6. Drink 30–40 drops three times a day, depending on the ailment and the plant you chose.

INFUSED OILS
AND UNGUENTS

$\cdot$ $\blacklozenge$ $\cdot$

*A*n infused oil is the product of a fresh or dry plant being macerated in oil, which is then used to make unguents. There are two ways to make an infused oil: double-boil, or the hot method, and by sunlight, or the cold method. The former is faster, but the latter will give you infused oils with the positive energy of the sun. The most commonly used oil for this preparation is cold-pressed sunflower-seed oil. For some traditional recipes, like Saint-John's-wort oil, olive oil is used.

Infused oils and unguents can be used for regenerative massages, compresses, lotions, and balms.

Double-boil method

This method is recommended mainly for dried herbs, especially spices or hot herbs, like turmeric, ginger, hot pepper, cinnamon, and cloves.

1. Crumple the herbs, and put them in a double boiler.
2. Cover the herbs with at least 0.8 inches (2 cm) of oil.
3. Let the herbs simmer slowly for at least an hour, making sure the oil does not burn.
4. Filter, squeeze the herbs out well, and store in a dark-glass jar in the dark.

Sunlight method

1. Put the crumpled herbs in a jar without stuffing it completely.
2. Cover the herbs with oil.
3. Close the jar, with cheesecloth if using fresh herbs or a lid if using dried herbs. Put the jar in the sunlight for at least 40 days.
4. Filter and bottle in dark-glass containers.

Unguent

1. Combine 8.4 fluid ounces (250 ml) of infused oil with 1.7 ounces (50 g) of beeswax—or candelilla wax for vegan versions—or, for a softer unguent, 3.5 ounces (100 g) of shea butter.
2. Heat in a double boiler until the wax is melted.
3. Let it cool, then add 20 drops of an essential oil of your choice (optional).
4. Put in small glass jars and let solidify; store in a cool, dry place.

HERBAL PILLS

Making herbal pills, a concentrated natural remedy, is easy and quick. You can take one to three pills a day when necessary.

1. Crush the herbs, put them in a dish, and add water and honey until the mixture becomes a thick paste.
2. Add one or two drops of essential oil (optional).
3. Add cacao or carob powder to solidify.
4. Make a pill shape with your hands.
5. Place in the oven at a low temperature, around 104°F (40°C), and let it dry completely.
6. Store in a glass jar.

FLOWER OR HERB VINEGAR

Keeping some vinegar flavored with flower petals, herbs, or wild fruits on hand is always useful: The vinegar is antibacterial, helps preserve foods and flavor them, and is an excellent solvent for herbs.

1. Fill a jar ¾ of the way full with crushed herbs, fruits, or fresh flowers and ¼ of the way full with spices or dried herbs.
2. Cover with vinegar: red or white wine vinegar or, my favorite, cider vinegar.
3. Close with a non-aluminum lid, or place a piece of wax paper under the lid.
4. Let it infuse in a cool, dry place for a month, checking in the first few days that the herbs are well covered by the vinegar.
5. Filter and store in a dark-glass jar.

FLORAL EXTRACT

• ♦ •

Flowers help bring balance to emotions. To assume their properties, we can extract the floral (chemical and energetic) essences with sunlight infusion by leaving them in water and setting them in direct sunlight.

STEP ONE: LOOK FOR FLOWERS

Look for a flower that attracts you near home—as long as it's an unpolluted place—or your favorite natural environment. Identify it. You must know with certainty that the flower you are harvesting is the one you want to use and that it can be used; do not experiment.

STEP TWO: PREPARE THE WATER

Once you have identified the place and plant, fill a dish with fresh (not distilled) water. Place the dish in a sunny place.

STEP THREE: PICK THE FLOWERS

Picking the flowers to make the floral essence is a magical gesture. Have an open and grateful attitude for the gift Mother Earth has given you.

The flowers should be gathered without touching them with your hands. Use a part of the plant, like a leaf, to pick them one by one. You can also use scissors and have them drop directly into the water.

Make sure not to cast shadows on the water. You should pay attention to your body and the sky; clouds should not pass by. If a shadow touches your infusion, you should start over.

The flowers must float on the surface of the water and remain exposed to the sun for at least three hours.

STEP FOUR: WAIT

You can spend the three hours reading a book, meditating and drawing flowers in your notebook, or taking pictures of the sky. You can invent a little ritual, burn some fragrant resin, make a mandala of flowers and leaves, or follow some ants and discover where they live. Talk to the birds. Make daisy crowns and wear them. Change your name. Make inspiring lists. Whatever you want!

STEP FIVE: PREPARE THE MOTHER BOTTLE

Remove the flowers from the dish without touching them by using a leaf or other plant material. Now you can pour the infused water in a bottle and add the same quantity of brandy. Use a scale to make this precise. This is the mother essence.

Label the bottle: Write the name of the flower, the date and the place it was made, and whatever else seems important to you (for example: "I could hear the titmouse chirp," "across the rainbow," "near a holed rock," and so on). From this mother bottle you can make stock bottles.

STOCK BOTTLES

The stock bottle is the bottle needed to make vials used for treatments. Take a 1 fluid ounce (30 ml) vial, and fill it with brandy. Add 2 drops of mother essence. Put a lid on the vial, and write the name of the remedy on the label, specifying that it is a stock bottle.

VIALS FOR TREATMENT

Take a 1 fluid ounce (30 ml) vial with a dropper, and fill it with pure water. Add a spoonful of brandy and 2 drops from the stock bottles for each type of remedy you want. If it is only one, add only 2 drops. From this vial you can take 4 drops four times a day directly in the mouth.

CHAPTER 7

FROM ROOT TO FLOWER: TAKING CARE OF YOUR GARDEN

I HAVE ALWAYS WANTED A GARDEN.
MY GRANDMOTHER WAS GIFTED
IN TAKING CARE OF PLANTS,
AND I REMEMBER AFTERNOONS
AS A CHILD AMONG HER ROSES,
FLOWERING GARLIC BULBS, AND VIOLETS
HIDDEN BETWEEN THE COBBLESTONES.

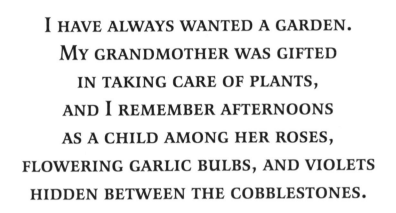

When I got older, I decided to live near a forest, and now I have the garden I'd always dreamed of. But taking care of a garden is possible also in the city, even if you don't have a green space. A garden is the place where you can relax, meditate, watch the seasons pass, and take care of your plants, making real contact with nature.

PLANNING
A GARDEN

♥ ♥ ♥

Taking care of a garden allows you to establish an exchange of energy with plants and the natural life cycle. If you live in a house without a garden, you can build one on your balcony with vases, little wood houses, and small seedbeds. You can even create one inside by choosing plants that live best indoors.

Then study the place you have chosen. What are the climate conditions like? Humidity? Sun exposure? Get a notebook, and write down all the information you find out in the place you have chosen and imagine you have to move there. You can also analyze the soil: Is it sandy, clay-based, acidic, basic? If you are creating your garden on a balcony, think about how you would place the vases, what vases you already have, and how you can use recycled containers for a more eco-friendly choice. You can take advantage of vertical space by using a planter, beautiful hanging pots, and so on.

Ask yourself what the point of your garden is. Do you want to grow flowers and pick fresh ones every morning, or do you like herbs and want a garden of fragrant medicinal plants? Or maybe you would prefer to grow your own vegetables, even on a balcony. Make a list of all the plants you would like to grow, and then check if the climate, sun exposure, and soil of your garden are good for this.

Remember to leave a small part of your garden uncultivated as a gift to Mother Earth and her wild spirit. This is a good way to invite fairies to pass through your garden.

PLANTING
WITH THE MOON

♥ ♥ ♥

In ancient times, people were already aware of the moon's influence on planting and growing. Almanacs, which even today contain advice and tricks for planting, derive their name from the Arabic word *al-manākh*. One of the functions of these books has always been to share practices for the garden based on the lunar phases.

And these are not just ancient beliefs, as biodynamic agriculture tells us. Scientific studies have verified the influence of the moon on seeds, sprouts, and the growth of plants.

More specifically, you should:

- Plant all plants that grow above ground, like tomatoes, eggplant, zucchini, and lettuce, during a phase of the moon. The strength of the waxing moon improves the germination of the seed and helps push the plants upward through the soil.

- Plant all plants that grow into the soil—potatoes, onions, garlic, turnips, and some types of lettuce, like endive—during a waning moon to avoid bolting.

It has also been proven that different parts of plants develop in sync with the changing signs of the moon. For example:

- When the moon is an earth sign, the roots develop better.
- When it is a fire sign, fruits, legumes, and cereal grains grow best.
- When it is an air sign, flowers and herbs thrive.
- When it is a water sign, leaves, stalks, and stems grow well.

Before planting or harvesting, take a look up at the sky!

TAKING CARE
OF PLANTS

❤ ❤ ❤

D eciding to introduce a plant, a small flower bed, a dozen vases, or a small garden is a way to bring someone new into your life. Your relationship and care for those plants become part of your daily life.

My most important piece of advice is to pursue natural methods in caring for your garden. You can make compost, natural fertilizer (there are even small compost bins for balconies), and infusions of sage and mint to keep insects away. If you'd like a natural garden, remember that the methods of care you use should follow this approach.

More specifically:

- Don't throw away all your waste when you cook. Fruit peels, coffee grounds, tea bags, eggshells, and vegetable remains are an excellent base for compost, to which you can add plant cuttings, noncolored paper, and soil.

- Keep a watchful eye on your plants every day. Pull yellow or withered leaves, check that they don't have insects, make sure the soil is well drained. This will help strengthen your tie with them and be aware of the natural passing of the seasons.

- Try to water your plants with different herbal infusions and see whether they have changed. Good infusions for improving the growth and health of plants include chamomile, yarrow, and nettle.

- Check the moon and seasons before planting, cutting, and harvesting.

Take a deck of tarot cards, and pull a card for your plant. The images on the card might reveal something about its voice and message for you.

PLANNER
The Work of the Green Witch According to the Magical Year

JANUARY

Take some time to plan your garden. Choose which seeds to plant, excluding those that haven't satisfied you. Pull weeds and clean your beds of various residues. Reorder your garden tools and hang bunches of yarrow in the shed to bring good fortune for the new plants. Plant tulip bulbs.

FEBRUARY

If you look carefully, you might find a few violets already blooming toward the end of the month. You can make a syrup with them. In the garden, transplant onion and garlic. It's time to plant lavender, thyme, cucumber, tomatoes, and eggplant in peat pots. Do so at the end of the month when the moon is waxing. Distribute ashes from the wood stove around the plants to ward off snails.

MARCH

With the spring equinox, the days will grow longer. Gather the first nettle tops for risotto and teas and tender dandelion leaves to sauté or add to salads. Pull the weeds that have survived the winter. Plant peas and fava beans outside and also sweet peas to please the fairies.

APRIL

When the moon is waning, dig holes in your beds and stick in the potatoes; then aerate the seedbeds and check on the strawberries.

You can get rid of aphids with a solution of water and Marseille soap. If you live in a cold region, plant cucumber, pepper, and basil indoors and arugula, radicchio, and spinach outdoors. Pick the strawberries, chard, parsley, and leek. During walks, you might find some wild asparagus.

MAY
Pick some roses, and dry them to add to teas or sugar as a fragrance. Dig up the peppers and put hay around the strawberries. Pick some marigolds for oil infusions. Water in the morning so that the plants don't burn. Finish transplanting: It's time to plant the tomatoes, eggplant, zucchini, peppers, and pumpkins and collect the first fruits. Pick mallow and chamomile for teas.

JUNE
Around the 24th, pick Saint-John's-wort for Saint John's feast day. Pick mint, lemon balm, thyme, rosemary, and other herbs just before flowering, and hang them to dry for teas, seasoning, and smudge sticks. Take cuttings from sage to multiply growth. Weed your garden every day, and continue harvesting. Plant late tomato and zucchini varieties that will fruit in autumn.

JULY
Remember to water your plants well. If you have peppers, tomatoes, zucchini, cucumber, and eggplant, use supports to hold them up, even with small branches from the woods. Pick sage and lavender flowers to dry for mothballs. Make unguents with marigolds and Saint-John's-wort. Pick fruits, and start making jam.

AUGUST
It's increasingly important to water the plants well, because there is often a lack of rain in this period. Till the soil around the vegetables to help the water soak in more deeply, and be sure to weed. Pick tomatoes for preserves with basil. With celery you can make tomato sauce. Pick plums with the stalk to help them stay fresh longer.

SEPTEMBER

Pick elderberries to make syrup and jam, which are excellent for coughs in the winter months. Trim trees that have no fruits, to help with summer growth. Dig holes to bury compost in flower beds without plants. Rake the first dry leaves into piles that can then be used as fertilizer the next year.

OCTOBER

Pick pumpkins. Put the more delicate plants inside, or cover with nonwoven fabric. You can make a delicate jam with hawthorn berries. Pick dog rose hips, cut them in two, take out the seeds, and dry them for winter teas. Pick apples and walnuts; hang a string of horse chestnuts in the closet to ward off moths.

NOVEMBER

Time slows, and we close ourselves off indoors. Trim fruit trees and pick the last chestnuts. Till the soil and bury compost. Prepare a talisman to protect your garden by braiding red string with three branches from a service or hazelnut tree. Study plants, and try the dried herbs in fragrant teas.

DECEMBER

Pick pine and spruce leaves for teas and restorative baths. If you are lucky enough to see mistletoe grow, gather a few branches to decorate your house and to create your Christmas tree. Leave a few sunflower and pumpkin seeds for the birds. You can roll them into small balls with butter and hang them in the trees to help them eat during the coldest days.

In every season, keep a wild heart.

January

1	9	17	25
2	10	18	26
3	11	19	27
4	12	20	28
5	13	21	29
6	14	22	30
7	15	23	31
8	16	24	

February

1	9	17	25
2	10	18	26
3	11	19	27
4	12	20	28
5	13	21	29
6	14	22	
7	15	23	
8	16	24	

March

1	9	17	25
2	10	18	26
3	11	19	27
4	12	20	28
5	13	21	29
6	14	22	30
7	15	23	31
8	16	24	

April

1	9	17	25
2	10	18	26
3	11	19	27
4	12	20	28
5	13	21	29
6	14	22	30
7	15	23	
8	16	24	

May

1	9	17	25
2	10	18	26
3	11	19	27
4	12	20	28
5	13	21	29
6	14	22	30
7	15	23	31
8	16	24	

June

1	9	17	25
2	10	18	26
3	11	19	27
4	12	20	28
5	13	21	29
6	14	22	30
7	15	23	
8	16	24	

July

1	9	17	25
2	10	18	26
3	11	19	27
4	12	20	28
5	13	21	29
6	14	22	30
7	15	23	31
8	16	24	

August

1	9	17	25
2	10	18	26
3	11	19	27
4	12	20	28
5	13	21	29
6	14	22	30
7	15	23	31
8	16	24	

September

1	9	17	25
2	10	18	26
3	11	19	27
4	12	20	28
5	13	21	29
6	14	22	30
7	15	23	
8	16	24	

October

1	9	17	25
2	10	18	26
3	11	19	27
4	12	20	28
5	13	21	29
6	14	22	30
7	15	23	31
8	16	24	

November

1	9	17	25
2	10	18	26
3	11	19	27
4	12	20	28
5	13	21	29
6	14	22	30
7	15	23	
8	16	24	

December

1	9	17	25
2	10	18	26
3	11	19	27
4	12	20	28
5	13	21	29
6	14	22	30
7	15	23	31
8	16	24	

TEST
WHAT TYPE OF WITCH ARE YOU?

1) If you had to choose a magic wand, it would be:
   A. A wooden spoon
   B. A fallen branch from a service tree
   C. A raven's feather with a little bell

2) Your favorite room of the house is:
   A. The kitchen, with the wood stove and bunches of herbs hanging upside down
   B. The bathroom, with unguents, perfumed oils, and little magic vials
   C. Room? What room? I'm in the garden as much as possible!

3) Your favorite herbal tea is:
   A. Marigold, lemon balm, mint, oregano, and rock candy
   B. Nettle, raspberry leaves, licorice powder, and two mugwort leaves
   C. A hot and energizing coffee made of acorn, chicory, and bitter herbs

4) Your witch's cape is:
   A. Red, like the flame in the wood stove
   B. Green, like freshly sprouted grass
   C. Brown, like the forest undergrowth at sunset

5) Your favorite magic spell is:
   A. Boil, boil, stir and simmer, complete the spell in this instant!
   B. By the sap that drips, the water that runs, the green of the woods, give me now what I ask for!
   C. No spell—just a murmured chant

• MOSTLY A

KITCHEN WITCH: You love to mix spells and soups with your wooden spoon while magic bread made of honey and sesame rises in the oven. If you still have room, I might join you for tea!

• MOSTLY B

GREEN WITCH: You're a classic Green Witch. You have a cupboard bursting with jars of herbs and at least eleven books about botany, where you can learn about plants and how to recognize them. Your favorite color is green, obviously.

• MOSTLY C

HEDGE WITCH: You didn't need this test to figure this out, right? You know the edge—the magic of the threshold—and you have a cat named Cagliostro, or something similar. Tonight I will watch the sky and say hello when you pass by on your broom.

10 MAGICAL STORIES
OF HERBS
AND WITCHES

HILDEGARD OF BINGEN

Viriditas and the curative power of herbs

....

Hildegard of Bingen was a medieval nun, visionary, herbalist, healer, mystic, theologian, cosmologist, and writer. She was a woman of many talents and had very realistic ideas about medicine and the cosmos for someone born in 1098. Hildegard dedicated her life to study, prayer, and contemplation. Some of her theories are found in natural medicine today. She was ahead of the times thanks to her visionary abilities. A brilliant aristocrat, Hildegard was able to study, which helped cultivate her eclectic spirit. She became known as an authority, consulted by bishops, popes, and kings. Hildegard noticed connections between all parts of the cosmos: human beings, plants, crystals, animals, and planets. She called this vital and verdant energy that feeds and unites everything *viriditas*. Illness is an indication of a break with the natural world and a loss of *viriditas*, or spiritual green energy. Hildegard studied illness according to the humoral discipline of Galen, combined with an exploration of emotions and the human mind, an early concept of psychosomatic theory. Hildegard used a totally innovative method to describe medicinal plants: In addition to discussing them from a botanical perspective, she explored their properties and their effects depending on the person consuming them—their sex, constitution, and medical history. Hildegard was also a musician and composer, and she took into consideration the power of sound and words. I like to think that plants chose her voice to speak to us, almost 1,000 years ago.

ELISA AND ANDERSEN'S WILD SWANS

Nettle

....

In the fields of Novgorod, Russia, children jump over bunches of stinging nettle on Saint John's Eve. The plant represents fire; its power is hot and dry, stinging and energizing, warrior-like and generous. It is said in central Europe that lightning never strikes nettle. In Tyrol, Austria, nettle is thrown on the hearth to ward off danger. In popular tradition, nettle is an aphrodisiac and helps with childbirth. It is connected to the generative aspect of life and is a plant of protection and strength.

Hans Christian Andersen was well aware of this symbolism. In his fairy tale *The Wild Swans*, nettle is a necessary tool used to break a spell and restore balance. Elisa is a princess with eleven brothers, who is adored by her father. Her stepmother, jealous of her kindness and beauty, pushes her away from her home and transforms her brothers into wild swans. After years of life on her own, Elisa meets an old woman in the woods who tells her about eleven swans that live nearby, each with a crown on its head. Elisa thus is reunited with her brothers, who are swans by day and men by night. In a dream, she finds out that in order to free them from the spell, she must gather stinging nettles with her bare hands and knit them together to create eleven magic shirts for her brothers. Elisa manages to complete the task and free her brothers with the shirts made of nettle, a plant that proves once again to be tenacious and magical.

THE HEALERS OF THE TUSCAN-EMILIAN APENNINES

Herbs of fear

....

In the Pistoia mountains, a region north of Florence, Italy, fear is a personified figure, often used to scare troublesome children. "If you misbehave, Fear will come and take you away!" Thus fear takes the form of the places they should not pass, with bewitched figures and ghosts. It's something real, tangible. We think of fear as something that emotionally strikes a person and develops from there. But fear is also felt physically, in our stomach that tightens, in our heart that beats faster, in our breathing that becomes labored. But there is a plant called the herb of fear (*Stachys recta*, or stiff hedgenettle), which has the magical and magnetic power to dissolve and push away fear.

Fear is washed away with an herbal tea made by boiling the herb in water and then washing the frightened person. The face, hands, and feet are washed while reciting ancient spells passed down through oral tradition. The water in the pot slowly solidifies and becomes gelatinous, or *borraccinoso*. Fear is transferred to the water. The washing is repeated two more times until the water runs clear. This ritual is still practiced by some elderly women, including my grandmother. This wisdom has been passed down from generation to generation. It keeps courage and magic alive and helps overcome fear.

RITUALS FOR SAINT JOHN'S FEAST DAY

Saint-John's-wort

....

S aint-John's-wort has its peak moment around the summer solstice, which precedes Saint John's Eve. It is said that the flower's purple color that stains your hands comes from the blood of Saint John. When walking through the woods, you can put a twig of it in your shirt along with garlic and rue to ward off witches who have gathered for the annual sabbat on Saint John's Eve. In many European countries, people put a crown of Saint-John's-wort around their head and dance barefoot around fires. The plant is supportive and brightening, just like the summer light.

It is a plant of maximum protection, used to drive away devils and evil presences. It is curative, soothing, and healing and tied to eternal youth.

The water ritual for Saint John's Eve recalls these traditions. On the night between June 23 and 24, flowers and herbs, like Saint-John's-wort, rosemary, mallow, lavender, and mullein, are gathered and placed in a dish of water to leave out under the light of the moon. In the morning, they are used to wash one's hands and face. This ensures beauty, fortune, and health for the coming year.

In some mountain regions in Italy, it is said that at dawn following Saint John's Eve, women dance nude among the bushes of Saint-John's-wort so that they may be covered in dew, which will help them remain young and beautiful.

QUEEN ISABELLA OF HUNGARY

Rosemary

....

Rosemary is one of the most common plants used for Saint John's water. It has many beneficial properties, which even ancient Egyptians were aware of. It was apparently associated with immortality, and they would leave a bunch next to the dead to help them on their journey to the afterlife. It is a powerful and purifying magical plant connected to life, fertility, and rebirth. In the nineteenth century in the countryside around Bologna, Italy, it was believed that carrying rosemary flowers against the skin, especially near the heart, brought happiness. Rosemary is closely connected to memory, and some people used to wear a crown of it while studying. In *Hamlet*, Ophelia said that rosemary is for remembrance.

Rosemary's magical power is why it's said to have great medicinal uses, like the famous water of the queen of Hungary. A recipe for the drug has been traced back to Isabella of Hungary. It was apparently given to her by a hermit—or an angel in disguise—to help cure her of gout and illness. In 1370, she began drinking the water at the age of seventy-two, and in one year she was once again so beautiful and glowing that the king of Poland asked her to marry him.

ARTEMIS AND THE QUEEN OF SNAKES

Mugwort

....

Mugwort is a lunar plant connected to femininity, child-birth, and the realm between the real world and the enchanted dreamworld. In *De herbarum virtutibus* by Pseudo Apuleius, it is said that the first mugwort was gathered by the goddess Artemis herself. It is called the herb of women because it cures any issue related to the female cycle, protects childbirth, and is believed to be an antidote to any poison. Artemis, a goddess with a fearless spirit, protects the woods, is devoted to sisterhood, and is found in this tough, fragrant plant that grows along the paths that lead to the heart of the woods.

One Ukrainian legend tells the story of a girl who, while picking mushrooms in the woods, falls into a hole that leads to an underground cave. Here lives the queen of snakes, with golden horns. The snakes lick a shining stone for sustenance. In order to remain hidden, the girl mimics the snakes and remains underground all winter. When spring arrives, the snakes turn themselves into stairs to help her get out and return to her world. The queen with golden horns, at this point, gives the girl the gift of knowing all the properties of herbs as long as she never says the name of mugwort. If she does, she will forget everything she has ever learned. One day, a man asks her the name of the plant growing on the path, and she says "mugwort"! She immediately forgets everything, and from that day mugwort is called the plant of forgetfulness.

AVALON, THE ISLAND OF APPLES, AND MORGAN LE FAY

Apples

....

One of the names for Avalon, the magic island where the enchantresses beloved by Arthur and Merlin lived, was Ynys Afallach, or island of apples, cited in *Historia regum Britanniae* by Geoffrey of Monmouth. There is a lot of symbolism surrounding apples. It is one of the fruits, along with pomegranate, most associated with the primordial Great Mother (or Triple Goddess), who was venerated in Avalon. In Arthurian legend, Morgan le Fay, a fairy and enchantress, and the Lady of the Lake are mythical creatures who live on this island. They reach it by walking through mist that hides it from humans. The island of apples is a paradise, where fruits and flowers grow without being cultivated and where apples are not eaten because they represent immortality. Apples are also connected to rebirth and are magical objects for transformative journeys. Snow White falls asleep when she takes a bite of an apple before being reborn with new life. The connection between apples and Morgan le Fay is related to the link between the fruit and the sacred feminine. The apple is offered as a gift to the Great Mother as a maid, mother, and crone, figures that follow the lunar phases—new, full, and waning. In Celtic traditions, the Great Mother was a wonderful maid who rode on a black horse while holding a golden apple.

When the apple is cut horizontally, there is a five-pointed star. This magic pentagram reminds us how the sacred is protected by the daily, even in small gestures, and how magic is truly all around us.

EMILY DICKINSON AND THE POETIC GARDEN

....

Before becoming a poet, Emily Dickinson was a botanist. She began building her wonderful little herbarium at nine years old. It would come to contain 424 plants, flowers, and herbs; today it's preserved in the Emily Dickinson Collection in the Houghton Library at Harvard University. Her poems are full of references to the plants she loved. Devoted to a life in seclusion, she rarely left her room, other than to go to the garden or greenhouse, where she grafted plants and grew peonies, daffodils, dahlias, lilies, and exotic plants. After starting Mount Holyoke school at fourteen, she began studying botany through the scientific method. In 1847, botany was the only way for women to access the sciences and academia. Mary Lyon, the founder of the school, was a botanist, and she encouraged her students to keep an herbarium. Emily presented her plants with extreme care and elegance and placed them with an acute sensibility for the beauty of nature. The first flower in her herbarium is jasmine, an exotic flower that combines purity and sensuality, just like her poems.

EVA MAMELI CALVINO AND SEEDS

....

Eva Mameli Calvino was a pioneer of the environmentalist movement. Born in 1886 in Sassari, on the Italian island of Sardinia, Eva was the mother of the famous writer Italo Calvino. As a girl, she enrolled in the public high school in Cagliari, the capital of Sardinia, which was traditionally all-male, before graduating with a degree in natural sciences in Pavia, in the north of Italy. There she started working with the Cryptogram Botany Laboratory, the only one in Italy that studied plant physiology and anatomy. She became a lab assistant, and after years of research, studies, and publications, she became the first woman in Italy to hold a university lectureship.

Eva later met Mario Calvino, director of the Agricultural Experiment Station in Santiago de las Vegas, Cuba. They married and left for Cuba, where Italo was born. There, Eva collected, cataloged, and conserved many seeds and opened a school to promote professional courses for girls on the island so that they might be emancipated. In 1925, the family returned to Italy. Mario became head of the Floriculture Experiment Station, which passed to Eva when he died. Eva brought kiwi, yucca, grapefruit, and palm variety seeds to Italy for the first time. Along with her husband, she founded a naturalist magazine, *Il Giardino Fiorito*, in which she wrote about the importance of protecting birds, among other issues. She died at ninety-two after a lifetime focused on caring for, cataloging, and spreading plants and their vital message.

CIRCE AND THE WOMEN OF HERBS

....

I dedicate this final story to Circe, as well as Medea and all the herbalist witches, healers, and wise women who have continued to transmit the magic and knowledge of plants since antiquity. They are all incarnations of the Potnia Theron, the Lady of Animals (and herbs)—manifestations of the Mother Goddess, who personifies the wild and free power of nature, protecting wild animals and spontaneous herbs. In short, the Lady of Nature herself. I see all herbalist women in Circe, those who understood herbs and healed the sick: the shaman at the edge of the woods, in her hut near the hedge, who offered cures and countercurses in exchange for gifts; obstetricians, midwives, and women who have cured other women for centuries; women who prepared love potions, who boiled willow bark to lower fevers, and who gathered Saint-John's-wort and mugwort on Saint John's Eve to ward off devils and protect from lightning; and wild, illiterate women who could recognize any wild plant, cook with nettle and dandelion, and prepare unguents to breathe better or for prophetic dreams.

The Potnia has never slept. She still lives in the heart of the woods, in the heart of every witch, in those who decide to follow the green path with humility, patience, light, and care. In those who know deep in their hearts that they want to become witches— because, as they know, all you have to do is remember. Remember you are one.

BIBLIOGRAPHY

Beth, Rae. *Hedge Witch: A Guide to Solitary Witchcraft.* London: Robert Hale, 1990.

Boland, Maureen, and Bridget Boland. *Old Wives' Lore for Gardeners.* London: Bodley Head, 2019.

Cattabiani, Alfredo. *Florario: Miti, leggende e simboli di fiori e piante.* Milan: Mondadori, 2017.

Cunningham, Scott. *Earth Power: Techniques of Natural Magic.* St. Paul, MN: Llewellyn Publications, 1983.

Cunningham, Scott. *Encyclopedia of Magical Herbs.* St. Paul, MN: Llewellyn Publications, 1985.

Emily Dickinson Collection. Houghton Library, Harvard Library. https://library.harvard.edu/collections/emily-dickinson-collection.

Fabbrini, Serena. "Eva Mameli Calvino, la maga buona che coltiva gli iris." *OggiScienza.* June 25, 2020. https://oggiscienza.it/2020/06/25/eva-mameli-calvino-maga-buona-coltiva-iris/.

Johnson, Cait. *Witch in the Kitchen: Magical Cooking for All Seasons.* Rochester, VT: Destiny Books, 2001.

Lapucci, Carlo, and Anna Maria Antoni. *Erbolario familiar: Storia e magia delle erbe.* Florence: Ponte alle Grazie, 1994.

Matarrese, Eleonora. *La cuoca selvatica: Storie e ricette per portare la natura in tavola.* Milan: Bompiani, 2018.

Matonti, Loredana. *Erbe e antichi rimedi di ieri, oggi e domain.* Borgone Susa: Graffio, 2015.

McBride, Kami. *The Herbal Kitchen: Bring Lasting Health to You and to Your Family with 50 Easy-To-Find Common Herbs and Over 250 Recipes.* Newburyport, MA: Conari Press, 2019.

Mel. "Le sacre terre delle mele e le sue divine custodi: Storie dell'Oltremondo dal Mediterraneo ad Avalon." *Sulle Sponde di Boscomadre.* June 24, 2020. https://spondediboscomadre.com/2020/06/24/lesacre-terre-delle-mele-e-le-sue-divine-custodi-storie-delloltremondodal-mediterraneo-ad-avalon/.

Moura, Ann [Aoumiel]. *Green Magic: The Sacred Connection to Nature.* St. Paul, MN: Llewellyn Publications, 2002.

Murphy-Hiscock, Arin. *The Green Witch: Your Complete Guide to the Natural Magic of Herbs, Flowers, Essential Oils, and More.* New York: Adams Media, 2017.

Rangoni, Laura. *Il grande libro delle piante magiche.* Pavia, Italy: Xenia Edizioni, 2005.

Roux, Jessica. *Floriography: An Illustrated Guide to the Victorian Language of Flowers.* Kansas City, MO: Andrews McMeel Publishing, 2020.

Saito, Carol. *Il giardino incantato di Hermione: Il manuale delle Streghe.* Verona: Italy: Cerchio della Luna, 2005.

Satanassi, Lucilla, and Hubert Bösch. *Petali e rugiada.* Quarto di Sarsina, Italy: Humus Edizioni, 2010.

Schulke, Daniel A. *Veneficium: Magic, Witchcraft and the Poison Path.* 2nd ed. Hercules, CA: Three Hands Press, 2018.

Scott, Devon. *I giardini incantati: Le piante e la magia lunare.* Rome: Venexia, 2006.

Toll, Maia. *The Illustrated Herbiary: Guidance and Rituals from 36 Bewitching Botanicals.* North Adams, MA: Storey Publishing, 2018.

Van de Car, Nikki. *Calming Magic: Enchanted Rituals for Peace, Clarity, and Creativity.* Philadelphia: Running Press, 2020.

Zaccaro Garau, Mattia. "L'erbario di Emily Dickinson: L'infinito di un giardino." *Intersezionale.* January 19, 2021. https://www.intersezionale.com/2021/01/19/lerbario-di-emily-dickinson-linfinitodi-un-giardino/.

CECILIA LATTARI. Cecilia is both an herbalist who studied at the University of Bologna and a professional actress who graduated from the Theater School of Bologna. She is a teacher of social pedagogy who works in both tangible and imaginary education through various media: writing, theater, contact with the natural world, and relationships of support. She works in the area of relationships, stimulating people's contact with their most authentic self through theater performance and the sensory experience of interacting with the world of plants.

She lives in a small town in the Tuscan Apennines in Italy, near the woods. The light of the moon shines right on her doorway, and quite often she can be found having long chats with the moon and her cats.

BETTI GRECO. Betti is an illustrator and graphic designer who works in publishing and communications. Her visual, colorful, and fantastic approaches are digital but have a solid background in painting and are constantly being experimented with. She lives in Salento, Apulia, Italy, and she loves spending time in nature, where she reenergizes between jobs and finds major artistic inspiration. Her wand is her paintbrush, and her magical power is her imagination. Reality is just a starting point for exploring the senses and drawing new worlds!